WOODLAND KINGDOM COLORING BOOK

65+ Whimsical Designs for Creativity & Relaxation

by Toshiyuki Fukuda

C&T PUBLISHING
Another Maker Inspired!

Various animals live in the forest.

Various trees and flowers grow in the forest.

In just such a forest, there is a wonderful palace that all the animals adore.

They often visit the palace to play, drink tea, and chat amongst themselves.

Sometimes, the animals even receive a gift to take home.

This coloring book is replete with the fun-filled lives of these animals and their forests.

Please feel free to use your favorite coloring materials. You can use anything from colored pencils to water-based pens to crayons, watercolors, and so on.

This book uses paper that doesn't bleed easily, which helps create truly beautiful coloring.

However, when painting with water-based pens or watercolors, it's best not to use many layers.

Overlaying water-based pens or watercolors will cause colors to bleed, even on the good-quality paper used here.

On another note, please feel free to decorate your works with your favorite masking tape or wrapping paper.

Be sure to use all of your imagination to complete your own coloring.

At the end, your own one-of-a-kind forest kingdom will surely appear.

This book includes three special circle-shaped coloring cards at the end.

You can color them as desired and then display them. Or you can write a message on the back and send them to someone special.

Let's go on a journey together to the Woodland Kingdom.

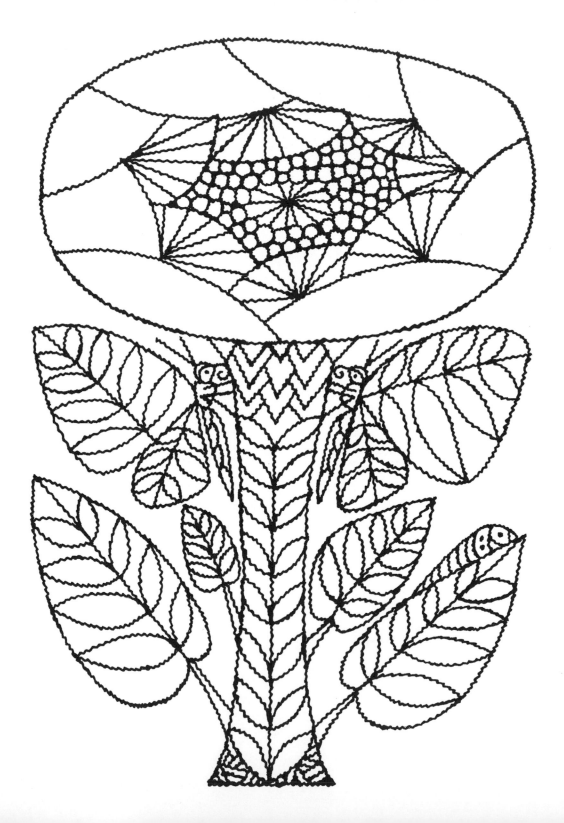

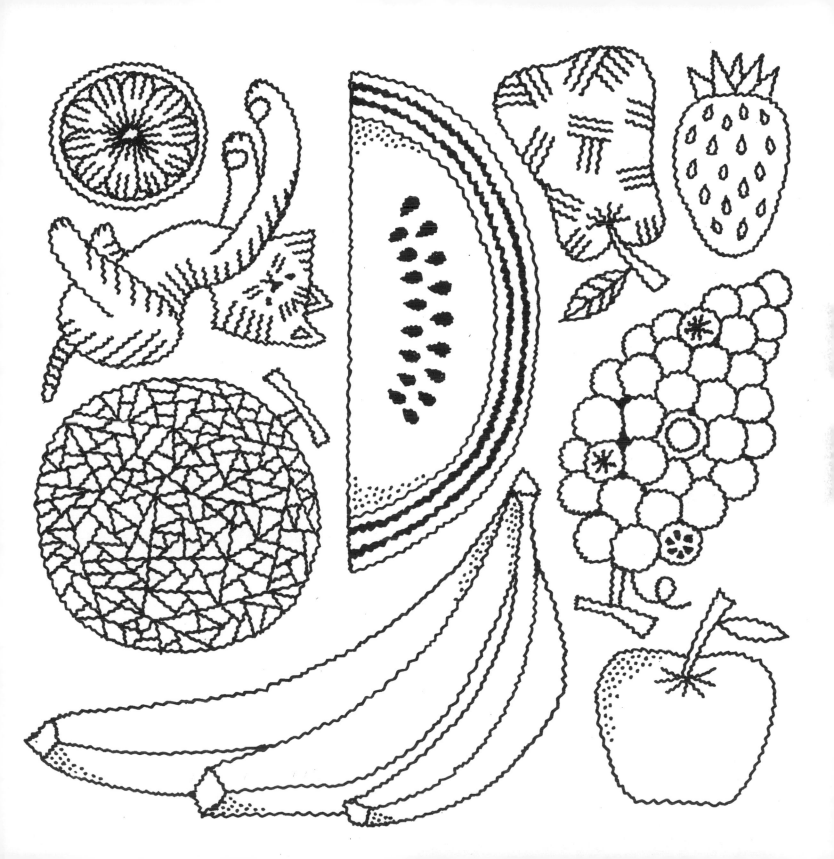

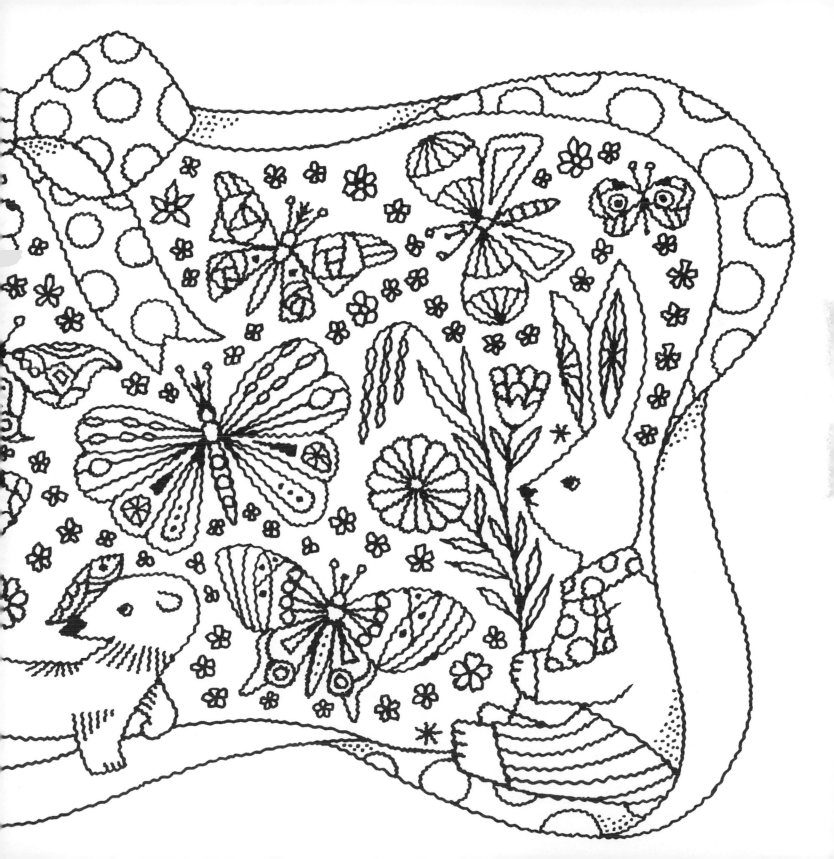

Toshiyuki Fukuda

Born in 1967, Fukuda is an illustrator based in Japan. He graduated from Osaka University of Arts, Department of Graphic Design. Fukuda works across various genres, including illustrations for CDs and books, children's books, and designing textiles. Major publications include *Toshiyuki Fukuda Works* (GENKOSHA), *Baby Book* (co-authored with Satoshi Fujimoto, KOKUYO ST), and *Boku wa Usagi (I Am a Rabbit)* (co-authored with Tetsu Yamashita, AKANE SHOBO).

http://www.to-fukuda.com

Woodland Kingdom Coloring Book

First published in the United States in 2023 by C&T Publishing, Inc., P.O. Box 1456, Lafayette, CA 94549

MORI NO OUKOKU FUKUDA TOSHIYUKI NURIE BOOK
© 2015 Toshiyuki Fukuda
© 2015 GRAPHIC-SHA PUBLISHING CO., LTD.
This book was first designed and published in Japan in 2015 by Graphic-sha Publishing Co., Ltd.
This English edition was published in 2023 by C&T PUBLISHING INC.
English language translation by Kevin Wilson
English translation rights arranged with GRAPHIC-SHA PUBLISHING CO., LTD. through Japan UNI Agency, Inc. and LibriSource Inc.
Original edition creative staff
Book design: Naoko Nakui
Editing: Junko Tsuda (Graphic-sha Publishing Co., Ltd.)
Foreign edition production and management: Takako Motoki (Graphic-sha Publishing Co., Ltd.)

PUBLISHER: Amy Barrett-Daffin
CREATIVE DIRECTOR: Gailen Runge
SENIOR EDITOR: Roxane Cerda
EDITOR: Jennifer Warren
ENGLISH-LANGUAGE COVER DESIGNER: Julie Creus
ENGLISH TRANSLATION: Kevin Wilson
PRODUCTION COORDINATOR: Zinnia Heinzmann
ILLUSTRATOR: Toshiyuki Fukuda

ISBN 978-1-64403-357-9

Printed in China

10 9 8 7 6 5 4 3 2 1